50 Restaurant Coffee Recipes for Home

By: Kelly Johnson

Table of Contents

- Classic Espresso
- Cappuccino
- Latte
- Americano
- Flat White
- Macchiato
- Mocha
- Irish Coffee
- Affogato
- Cold Brew Coffee
- Nitro Coffee
- Espresso Martini
- Caramel Macchiato
- Vanilla Latte
- Cinnamon Latte
- Hazelnut Coffee
- Almond Milk Latte
- Iced Coffee
- Coffee Milkshake
- Espresso Affogato
- Espresso Con Panna
- Café au Lait
- Coffee Mocha Milkshake
- Tiramisu Latte
- Coffee Float
- Cardamom Coffee
- Dalgona Coffee
- Café Cubano
- Turkish Coffee
- Vietnamese Iced Coffee
- Cold Brew Tonic
- Coffee Lemonade

- White Chocolate Mocha
- Spiced Coffee
- Coffee Egg Cream
- Coffee Smoothie
- Pumpkin Spice Latte
- Peppermint Mocha
- Hazelnut Cream Coffee
- Cinnamon Roll Coffee
- Maple Pecan Latte
- Gingerbread Latte
- Mocha Nutella Coffee
- Salted Caramel Latte
- Espresso Lemonade
- Café au Lait Affogato
- Coffee and Whiskey Cocktail
- Maple Cinnamon Coffee
- Chocolate Coconut Coffee
- Espresso Coconut Milk Latte

Classic Espresso

Ingredients:

- Freshly ground espresso coffee beans
- Water

Equipment:

- Espresso machine
- Coffee grinder (if using whole beans)

Instructions:

1. **Preheat Espresso Machine:** Turn on your espresso machine and allow it to fully preheat. This usually takes about 15-20 minutes.
2. **Grind Coffee Beans:** Grind your coffee beans to a fine consistency, specifically for espresso. You'll need about 18-20 grams of coffee for a double shot.
3. **Prepare Portafilter:** Place the portafilter on the scale and add the ground coffee. Level the coffee grounds and tamp them down evenly and firmly with a tamper. The coffee should be packed down with about 30 pounds of pressure.
4. **Brew Espresso:** Lock the portafilter into the espresso machine. Start the brewing process. A typical shot of espresso should take about 25-30 seconds to brew and yield about 1 ounce (30 ml) of espresso.
5. **Serve:** Once brewed, pour the espresso into a small cup and serve immediately. You can enjoy it as is or use it as a base for other coffee drinks.

Enjoy your classic espresso!

Cappuccino

Ingredients:

- 1 shot of espresso (about 1 ounce)
- 1/2 cup whole milk (or your preferred milk)
- 1/2 cup milk foam

Equipment:

- Espresso machine with a steam wand
- Coffee grinder (if using whole beans)
- Milk frother (if your espresso machine doesn't have a steam wand)

Instructions:

1. **Prepare Espresso:**
    - Grind your coffee beans to a fine consistency suitable for espresso. Use about 18-20 grams of coffee for a double shot.
    - Preheat your espresso machine and brew a shot of espresso into a cup.
2. **Froth the Milk:**
    - Heat the milk using the steam wand on your espresso machine or a separate milk frother. Heat until the milk reaches about 150°F (65°C).
    - Froth the milk until you have a creamy, velvety texture with a good amount of foam. You're aiming for a ratio of about 1/3 milk, 1/3 milk foam, and 1/3 air.
3. **Assemble the Cappuccino:**
    - Pour the hot milk into the cup with the espresso. Hold back the foam with a spoon and then spoon the foam on top of the milk.
4. **Serve:**
    - Optionally, you can sprinkle some cocoa powder or cinnamon on top of the foam for extra flavor. Serve immediately.

Enjoy your classic cappuccino!

Latte

Ingredients:

- 1 shot of espresso (about 1 ounce)
- 1 cup whole milk (or your preferred milk)

Equipment:

- Espresso machine with a steam wand
- Coffee grinder (if using whole beans)
- Milk frother (if your espresso machine doesn't have a steam wand)

Instructions:

1. **Prepare Espresso:**
    - Grind your coffee beans to a fine consistency for espresso. Use about 18-20 grams of coffee for a double shot.
    - Preheat your espresso machine and brew a shot of espresso into a cup.
2. **Froth the Milk:**
    - Heat the milk using the steam wand on your espresso machine or a separate milk frother. Heat until the milk reaches about 150°F (65°C).
    - Froth the milk until it's creamy and has a small amount of microfoam on top. The milk should have a smooth, velvety texture without large bubbles.
3. **Assemble the Latte:**
    - Pour the hot milk into the cup with the espresso. Start by pouring the milk from a bit of height to mix it with the espresso, then lower the pitcher and pour more slowly to create a layer of foam on top.
    - If you like, you can use a spoon to hold back the foam while pouring the milk, and then spoon the foam on top.
4. **Serve:**
    - Optionally, you can sprinkle a bit of cocoa powder, cinnamon, or nutmeg on top for extra flavor. Serve immediately.

Enjoy your classic latte!

Americano

Ingredients:

- 1 shot of espresso (about 1 ounce)
- 6-8 ounces hot water

Equipment:

- Espresso machine
- Coffee grinder (if using whole beans)
- Kettle or hot water source

Instructions:

1. **Prepare Espresso:**
    - Grind your coffee beans to a fine consistency suitable for espresso. Use about 18-20 grams of coffee for a double shot.
    - Preheat your espresso machine and brew a shot of espresso into a cup.
2. **Heat Water:**
    - Heat water to just below boiling, about 200°F (93°C). You can use a kettle or a hot water dispenser.
3. **Combine Espresso and Water:**
    - Pour the hot water into the cup with the brewed espresso. The typical ratio is 6-8 ounces of hot water for one shot of espresso, but you can adjust to taste.
4. **Serve:**
    - Stir gently and enjoy your Americano. You can adjust the strength by adding more or less water, depending on your preference.

Enjoy your Americano, which has a similar strength to drip coffee but with the rich flavor of espresso!

Flat White

Ingredients:

- 1 shot of espresso (about 1 ounce)
- 4-5 ounces whole milk (or your preferred milk)

Equipment:

- Espresso machine with a steam wand
- Coffee grinder (if using whole beans)
- Milk frother (if your espresso machine doesn't have a steam wand)

Instructions:

1. **Prepare Espresso:**
   - Grind your coffee beans to a fine consistency for espresso. Use about 18-20 grams of coffee for a double shot.
   - Preheat your espresso machine and brew a shot of espresso into a cup.
2. **Froth the Milk:**
   - Heat the milk using the steam wand on your espresso machine or a separate milk frother. Heat until the milk reaches about 150°F (65°C).
   - Froth the milk until it has a velvety texture with very fine microfoam. Unlike a latte, the milk should be less frothy and more integrated with the coffee.
3. **Assemble the Flat White:**
   - Pour the hot milk into the cup with the espresso, starting from a bit of height to mix the milk with the espresso, then lower the pitcher to create a creamy, smooth layer of microfoam on top. The goal is a silky, smooth finish with a small, even layer of foam.
4. **Serve:**
   - Optionally, you can use a toothpick or a skewer to create a latte art design on top.

Enjoy your flat white, a creamy and intense coffee experience with a perfect balance of espresso and microfoam!

Macchiato

Ingredients:

- 1 shot of espresso (about 1 ounce)
- A small amount of steamed milk or milk foam (optional, for traditional macchiato)

Equipment:

- Espresso machine
- Coffee grinder (if using whole beans)
- Milk frother (if you're adding milk foam)

Instructions:

1. **Prepare Espresso:**
    - Grind your coffee beans to a fine consistency suitable for espresso. Use about 18-20 grams of coffee for a double shot.
    - Preheat your espresso machine and brew a shot of espresso into a small cup.
2. **Add Milk (Optional):**
    - For a traditional macchiato, no milk is added, but if you prefer a slight touch of milk, steam a small amount of milk or froth a little milk foam.
    - Gently spoon a small dollop of the milk foam onto the espresso if using.
3. **Serve:**
    - Serve immediately. The term "macchiato" means "stained" or "spotted" in Italian, so traditionally the macchiato is just a shot of espresso with a small amount of milk foam or a touch of steamed milk.

Enjoy your classic macchiato, which highlights the bold flavor of espresso with just a hint of milk if desired!

Mocha

Ingredients:

- 1 shot of espresso (about 1 ounce)
- 1 cup whole milk (or your preferred milk)
- 2 tbsp cocoa powder
- 2 tbsp granulated sugar
- 2 tbsp hot water
- Whipped cream (optional, for topping)
- Chocolate shavings or cocoa powder (optional, for garnish)

Instructions:

1. **Prepare Cocoa Syrup:**
   - In a small bowl, mix the cocoa powder, sugar, and hot water to form a smooth chocolate syrup.
2. **Prepare Espresso:**
   - Grind your coffee beans to a fine consistency for espresso. Use about 18-20 grams of coffee for a double shot.
   - Preheat your espresso machine and brew a shot of espresso into a cup.
3. **Froth the Milk:**
   - Heat the milk using the steam wand on your espresso machine or a separate milk frother. Heat until the milk reaches about 150°F (65°C), and froth it until you get a creamy texture.
4. **Combine Ingredients:**
   - Pour the chocolate syrup into the cup with the brewed espresso and stir to combine.
   - Add the hot frothed milk to the cup and stir gently.
5. **Serve:**
   - Top with whipped cream, if desired, and garnish with chocolate shavings or a dusting of cocoa powder.

Enjoy your mocha, a delightful blend of rich chocolate and espresso!

Irish Coffee

Ingredients:

- 1 cup hot brewed coffee
- 1 1/2 oz Irish whiskey
- 1-2 tbsp brown sugar (to taste)
- Heavy cream (lightly whipped)
- Optional: cocoa powder or chocolate shavings (for garnish)

Instructions:

1. **Prepare Coffee:**
    - Brew a cup of hot coffee using your preferred method.
2. **Mix Whiskey and Sugar:**
    - In a heat-resistant glass or mug, combine the hot coffee with the Irish whiskey and brown sugar. Stir well until the sugar is completely dissolved.
3. **Top with Cream:**
    - Lightly whip the heavy cream until it's just thickened but still pourable.
    - Gently pour the cream over the back of a spoon to float it on top of the coffee. The goal is to have the cream float on top rather than mix into the coffee.
4. **Garnish (Optional):**
    - For a finishing touch, you can sprinkle a little cocoa powder or add chocolate shavings on top of the cream.
5. **Serve:**
    - Serve immediately and enjoy!

Irish Coffee is a wonderful blend of rich coffee and smooth whiskey, topped with a layer of creamy goodness.

Affogato

Ingredients:

- 1-2 scoops vanilla ice cream (or your preferred flavor)
- 1 shot of espresso (about 1 ounce)
- Optional: chocolate shavings or a splash of liqueur (e.g., amaretto)

Instructions:

1. **Prepare Espresso:**
    - Grind your coffee beans to a fine consistency for espresso. Use about 18-20 grams of coffee for a double shot.
    - Preheat your espresso machine and brew a shot of espresso into a small cup.
2. **Serve Ice Cream:**
    - Place 1-2 scoops of vanilla ice cream into a serving glass or bowl.
3. **Pour Espresso:**
    - Pour the hot espresso over the ice cream. The espresso should be hot enough to melt the ice cream slightly and create a delicious blend.
4. **Optional Garnish:**
    - For extra flavor, you can add chocolate shavings on top or a splash of liqueur if desired.
5. **Serve Immediately:**
    - Serve immediately while the ice cream is melting into the espresso.

Enjoy the delightful contrast between the creamy ice cream and the rich, hot espresso!

Cold Brew Coffee

Ingredients:

- 1 cup coarsely ground coffee beans
- 4 cups cold water

Equipment:

- Large jar or pitcher
- Fine mesh strainer or cheesecloth
- Coffee filter (optional)

Instructions:

1. **Combine Coffee and Water:**
    - In a large jar or pitcher, mix the coarsely ground coffee beans with the cold water. Stir to ensure all the coffee grounds are saturated.
2. **Steep:**
    - Cover the jar or pitcher and let it steep in the refrigerator for 12-24 hours. The longer it steeps, the stronger the flavor.
3. **Strain:**
    - After steeping, strain the coffee through a fine mesh strainer or cheesecloth into a clean container. For a smoother result, you can strain it again through a coffee filter.
4. **Serve:**
    - Dilute with water or milk to taste, if desired, and serve over ice.
5. **Store:**
    - Store any leftover cold brew concentrate in the refrigerator for up to two weeks.

Enjoy your refreshing cold brew coffee, perfect for a cool and energizing drink!

Nitro Coffee

Ingredients:

- Cold brew coffee (see recipe above)
- Nitrogen gas (from a nitro coffee dispenser or a whipped cream dispenser with N2 cartridges)

Equipment:

- Cold brew coffee
- Nitro coffee dispenser or whipped cream dispenser with N2 cartridges
- Coffee filter (optional)

Instructions:

1. **Prepare Cold Brew:**
   - Brew and strain cold brew coffee as per the recipe.
2. **Fill Dispenser:**
   - Pour the cold brew coffee into the nitro coffee dispenser or whipped cream dispenser.
3. **Add Nitrogen:**
   - If using a nitro coffee dispenser, follow the manufacturer's instructions to charge the coffee with nitrogen. If using a whipped cream dispenser, attach the N2 cartridge, shake well, and allow the coffee to infuse with nitrogen.
4. **Serve:**
   - Dispense the nitro coffee into a glass. The nitrogen infusion will create a creamy, frothy head on the coffee.
5. **Enjoy:**
   - Serve immediately to enjoy the smooth, effervescent texture of nitro coffee.

Nitro coffee offers a rich, creamy mouthfeel and a unique, refreshing twist on traditional cold brew!

Espresso Martini

Ingredients:

- 1 shot of fresh espresso (about 1 ounce)
- 1 1/2 oz vodka
- 1 oz coffee liqueur (e.g., Kahlúa)
- 1/2 oz simple syrup (adjust to taste)
- Ice
- Coffee beans (for garnish, optional)

Instructions:

1. **Prepare Espresso:**
    - Brew a shot of espresso and let it cool slightly.
2. **Mix Ingredients:**
    - In a cocktail shaker, combine the espresso, vodka, coffee liqueur, and simple syrup.
3. **Shake:**
    - Fill the shaker with ice and shake vigorously for about 15-20 seconds until well chilled and frothy.
4. **Strain:**
    - Strain the mixture into a chilled martini glass.
5. **Garnish:**
    - Garnish with a few coffee beans on top, if desired.

Enjoy your Espresso Martini, a sophisticated blend of coffee and cocktail for a perfect pick-me-up!

Caramel Macchiato

Ingredients:

- 1 shot of espresso (about 1 ounce)
- 1 cup whole milk (or your preferred milk)
- 2 tbsp vanilla syrup
- Caramel sauce (for drizzling)

Instructions:

1. **Prepare Espresso:**
    - Grind your coffee beans to a fine consistency for espresso. Use about 18-20 grams of coffee for a double shot.
    - Brew a shot of espresso and set aside.
2. **Froth the Milk:**
    - Heat the milk using the steam wand on your espresso machine or a separate milk frother until it reaches about 150°F (65°C), and froth until creamy and smooth.
3. **Assemble the Drink:**
    - Pour the vanilla syrup into the bottom of a cup.
    - Add the frothed milk, holding back the foam with a spoon.
    - Pour the shot of espresso over the top of the milk, allowing it to mix slightly but remain mostly layered.
4. **Drizzle with Caramel:**
    - Drizzle caramel sauce over the top of the milk and espresso.
5. **Serve:**
    - Serve immediately and enjoy!

The Caramel Macchiato is a delightful blend of sweet vanilla and rich caramel, topped with a bold espresso flavor.

Vanilla Latte

Ingredients:

- 1 shot of espresso (about 1 ounce)
- 1 cup whole milk (or your preferred milk)
- 1-2 tbsp vanilla syrup (adjust to taste)
- Optional: whipped cream and vanilla extract (for garnish)

Instructions:

1. **Prepare Espresso:**
    - Grind your coffee beans to a fine consistency for espresso. Use about 18-20 grams of coffee for a double shot.
    - Preheat your espresso machine and brew a shot of espresso into a cup.
2. **Froth the Milk:**
    - Heat the milk using the steam wand on your espresso machine or a separate milk frother until it reaches about 150°F (65°C). Froth until you achieve a creamy texture with a small amount of microfoam.
3. **Add Vanilla Syrup:**
    - Pour the vanilla syrup into the bottom of your cup.
4. **Combine Ingredients:**
    - Pour the hot, frothed milk over the vanilla syrup in the cup.
    - Add the brewed espresso to the cup.
5. **Optional Garnish:**
    - Top with whipped cream and a drizzle of vanilla extract or a sprinkle of vanilla bean powder, if desired.
6. **Serve:**
    - Serve immediately and enjoy your creamy Vanilla Latte!

This Vanilla Latte offers a delightful balance of sweet vanilla and bold espresso, perfect for a comforting beverage.

Cinnamon Latte

Ingredients:

- 1 shot of espresso (about 1 ounce)
- 1 cup whole milk (or your preferred milk)
- 1-2 tbsp cinnamon syrup (adjust to taste)
- Ground cinnamon (for garnish)

Instructions:

1. **Prepare Espresso:**
    - Grind your coffee beans to a fine consistency for espresso. Use about 18-20 grams of coffee for a double shot.
    - Preheat your espresso machine and brew a shot of espresso into a cup.
2. **Froth the Milk:**
    - Heat the milk using the steam wand on your espresso machine or a separate milk frother until it reaches about 150°F (65°C). Froth until creamy and smooth.
3. **Add Cinnamon Syrup:**
    - Pour the cinnamon syrup into the bottom of your cup.
4. **Combine Ingredients:**
    - Pour the frothed milk over the cinnamon syrup in the cup.
    - Add the brewed espresso to the cup.
5. **Garnish:**
    - Sprinkle a dash of ground cinnamon on top of the foam.
6. **Serve:**
    - Serve immediately and enjoy your aromatic Cinnamon Latte!

This Cinnamon Latte combines the warmth of cinnamon with the smoothness of a latte, creating a cozy and flavorful drink.

Hazelnut Coffee

Ingredients:

- 1 cup brewed coffee
- 2 tbsp hazelnut syrup or hazelnut flavoring (adjust to taste)
- 1-2 tbsp cream or milk (optional, for creaminess)
- Whipped cream (optional, for topping)
- Chopped hazelnuts (optional, for garnish)

Instructions:

1. **Brew Coffee:**
   - Brew a cup of coffee using your preferred method.
2. **Add Hazelnut Syrup:**
   - Stir in the hazelnut syrup or hazelnut flavoring. Adjust the amount based on your taste preference.
3. **Add Cream or Milk (Optional):**
   - For added creaminess, stir in 1-2 tablespoons of cream or milk.
4. **Serve:**
   - Pour the hazelnut coffee into a cup.
5. **Optional Toppings:**
   - Top with whipped cream if desired and sprinkle with chopped hazelnuts for extra flavor and texture.

Enjoy your Hazelnut Coffee, a delightful blend of nutty sweetness and rich coffee flavor!

Almond Milk Latte

Ingredients:

- 1 shot of espresso (about 1 ounce)
- 1 cup almond milk
- 1-2 tbsp almond syrup (optional, for extra almond flavor)
- Optional: ground almonds or a sprinkle of cinnamon (for garnish)

Instructions:

1. **Prepare Espresso:**
   - Grind your coffee beans to a fine consistency for espresso. Use about 18-20 grams of coffee for a double shot.
   - Preheat your espresso machine and brew a shot of espresso into a cup.
2. **Froth Almond Milk:**
   - Heat the almond milk using the steam wand on your espresso machine or a separate milk frother until it reaches about 150°F (65°C). Froth until creamy.
3. **Add Almond Syrup (Optional):**
   - If you like a stronger almond flavor, stir in 1-2 tablespoons of almond syrup into the brewed espresso.
4. **Combine Ingredients:**
   - Pour the hot, frothed almond milk over the espresso.
5. **Garnish (Optional):**
   - Top with a sprinkle of ground almonds or cinnamon for added flavor.
6. **Serve:**
   - Serve immediately and enjoy your nutty, creamy Almond Milk Latte!

This latte combines the smooth, nutty taste of almond milk with the rich flavor of espresso for a delightful beverage.

Iced Coffee

Ingredients:

- 1 cup brewed coffee (cooled)
- 1/2 cup ice cubes
- 1-2 tbsp sugar or simple syrup (adjust to taste)
- Milk or cream (optional, to taste)
- Optional: flavored syrups (e.g., vanilla, caramel) for extra flavor

Instructions:

1. **Brew Coffee:**
   - Brew a cup of coffee using your preferred method. Let it cool to room temperature or refrigerate it to speed up the process.
2. **Sweeten Coffee (Optional):**
   - If you like your coffee sweetened, stir in sugar or simple syrup while the coffee is still warm to ensure it dissolves completely. If you prefer, you can also use flavored syrups at this stage.
3. **Prepare Glass:**
   - Fill a glass with ice cubes.
4. **Pour Coffee:**
   - Pour the cooled coffee over the ice.
5. **Add Milk or Cream (Optional):**
   - Add milk or cream to taste if you like a creamier coffee. You can also use alternatives like almond milk, oat milk, or half-and-half.
6. **Serve:**
   - Stir well and serve immediately.

Enjoy your Iced Coffee, perfect for a cool and energizing drink on a warm day!

Coffee Milkshake

Ingredients:

- 1 cup brewed coffee (cooled)
- 2 cups vanilla ice cream
- 1/2 cup milk (or adjust for desired thickness)
- 1-2 tbsp sugar or simple syrup (optional, to taste)
- Whipped cream (optional, for topping)
- Chocolate or caramel syrup (optional, for drizzling)

Instructions:

1. **Prepare Coffee:**
   - Brew a cup of coffee and let it cool to room temperature.
2. **Blend Ingredients:**
   - In a blender, combine the cooled coffee, vanilla ice cream, milk, and sugar or simple syrup if desired. Blend until smooth.
3. **Serve:**
   - Pour the milkshake into a glass.
4. **Optional Toppings:**
   - Top with whipped cream and drizzle with chocolate or caramel syrup for extra indulgence.
5. **Enjoy:**
   - Serve immediately with a straw.

This Coffee Milkshake blends rich coffee flavor with creamy vanilla ice cream for a delightful treat!

Espresso Affogato

Ingredients:

- 1-2 scoops vanilla ice cream (or your preferred flavor)
- 1 shot of espresso (about 1 ounce)
- Optional: chocolate shavings, caramel sauce, or a splash of liqueur (e.g., amaretto)

Instructions:

1. **Prepare Espresso:**
    - Brew a shot of espresso and let it cool slightly if needed.
2. **Scoop Ice Cream:**
    - Place 1-2 scoops of vanilla ice cream into a serving glass or bowl.
3. **Pour Espresso:**
    - Pour the hot espresso directly over the ice cream. The hot espresso will slightly melt the ice cream, creating a creamy and delicious blend.
4. **Optional Toppings:**
    - For added flavor, you can sprinkle chocolate shavings on top or drizzle with caramel sauce.
    - For a grown-up twist, you can add a splash of liqueur, such as amaretto, over the espresso before pouring it over the ice cream.
5. **Serve:**
    - Serve immediately and enjoy the delightful contrast between the hot espresso and the cold, creamy ice cream.

This Espresso Affogato combines the rich flavor of espresso with the sweet, creamy texture of ice cream for a simple yet luxurious dessert.

Espresso Con Panna

Ingredients:

- 1 shot of espresso (about 1 ounce)
- Whipped cream (freshly whipped or from a can)

Instructions:

1. **Prepare Espresso:**
    - Grind your coffee beans to a fine consistency suitable for espresso. Use about 18-20 grams of coffee for a double shot.
    - Preheat your espresso machine and brew a shot of espresso into a small cup.
2. **Top with Whipped Cream:**
    - Generously top the hot espresso with a dollop of whipped cream. The whipped cream should be lightly sweetened to complement the bitterness of the espresso.
3. **Serve:**
    - Serve immediately, while the whipped cream is still soft and the espresso is hot.

Optional:

- For added flavor, you can sprinkle a little cocoa powder or cinnamon on top of the whipped cream.
- You can also drizzle a bit of caramel or chocolate sauce over the whipped cream for extra indulgence.

Espresso Con Panna is a simple yet elegant dessert that highlights the contrast between the rich, bold espresso and the creamy, sweet whipped cream.

Café au Lait

Ingredients:

- 1 cup brewed coffee
- 1 cup whole milk (or your preferred milk)

Instructions:

1. **Brew Coffee:**
   - Brew a cup of strong coffee using your preferred method (drip coffee maker, French press, etc.).
2. **Heat and Froth Milk:**
   - Heat the milk using a steam wand on your espresso machine, a milk frother, or on the stove until it reaches about 150°F (65°C).
   - Froth the milk until it's creamy and has a small amount of microfoam.
3. **Combine Coffee and Milk:**
   - Pour the brewed coffee into a large cup.
   - Add the hot, frothed milk to the coffee. You can adjust the ratio of coffee to milk based on your taste preference, but traditionally it's equal parts coffee and milk.
4. **Serve:**
   - Serve immediately.

Optional:

- You can sprinkle a bit of cocoa powder, cinnamon, or nutmeg on top for extra flavor.

Café au Lait is a comforting coffee drink with a balanced blend of rich coffee and creamy milk, perfect for starting your day or enjoying as an afternoon treat.

Coffee Mocha Milkshake

Ingredients:

- 1 cup brewed coffee (cooled)
- 2 cups chocolate ice cream
- 1/2 cup milk (adjust for desired thickness)
- 1-2 tbsp chocolate syrup
- Whipped cream (optional, for topping)
- Chocolate shavings or cocoa powder (optional, for garnish)

Instructions:

1. **Prepare Coffee:**
    - Brew a cup of coffee and let it cool to room temperature or chill it in the refrigerator.
2. **Blend Ingredients:**
    - In a blender, combine the cooled coffee, chocolate ice cream, milk, and chocolate syrup. Blend until smooth and creamy.
3. **Serve:**
    - Pour the milkshake into a glass.
4. **Optional Toppings:**
    - Top with whipped cream if desired, and garnish with chocolate shavings or a dusting of cocoa powder.
5. **Enjoy:**
    - Serve immediately with a straw.

This Coffee Mocha Milkshake combines the rich flavors of coffee and chocolate ice cream for a deliciously indulgent treat!

Tiramisu Latte

Ingredients:

- 1 shot of espresso (about 1 ounce)
- 1 cup whole milk (or your preferred milk)
- 1-2 tbsp tiramisu syrup or flavored coffee syrup (for a tiramisu flavor)
- Cocoa powder or chocolate shavings (for garnish)
- Optional: mascarpone cheese (for a richer flavor)

Instructions:

1. **Prepare Espresso:**
    - Grind your coffee beans to a fine consistency suitable for espresso. Use about 18-20 grams of coffee for a double shot.
    - Brew a shot of espresso and set aside.
2. **Froth the Milk:**
    - Heat the milk using a steam wand on your espresso machine or a separate milk frother until it reaches about 150°F (65°C). Froth until creamy.
3. **Add Tiramisu Flavor:**
    - Stir the tiramisu syrup or flavored coffee syrup into the brewed espresso. If using mascarpone cheese, blend a small amount into the syrup for added richness.
4. **Combine Ingredients:**
    - Pour the flavored espresso into a cup.
    - Add the hot, frothed milk.
5. **Garnish:**
    - Dust the top with cocoa powder or sprinkle with chocolate shavings.
6. **Serve:**
    - Serve immediately and enjoy your Tiramisu Latte!

This latte captures the rich, creamy essence of tiramisu, combining it with the boldness of espresso and the smoothness of frothed milk.

Coffee Float

Ingredients:

- 1 cup brewed coffee (cooled)
- 1-2 scoops vanilla ice cream
- Whipped cream (optional, for topping)
- Chocolate or caramel syrup (optional, for drizzling)

Instructions:

1. **Prepare Coffee:**
   - Brew a cup of coffee and let it cool to room temperature or refrigerate it to chill faster.
2. **Add Ice Cream:**
   - Place 1-2 scoops of vanilla ice cream into a glass.
3. **Pour Coffee:**
   - Gently pour the chilled coffee over the ice cream.
4. **Optional Toppings:**
   - Top with whipped cream and drizzle with chocolate or caramel syrup if desired.
5. **Serve:**
   - Serve immediately with a straw or spoon.

This Coffee Float combines the rich flavor of coffee with the creamy sweetness of ice cream for a refreshing and indulgent treat!

Cardamom Coffee

Ingredients:

- 1 cup brewed coffee
- 1/4 tsp ground cardamom (adjust to taste)
- 1-2 tbsp sugar (optional, to taste)
- Milk or cream (optional, to taste)

Instructions:

1. **Brew Coffee:**
    - Brew a cup of coffee using your preferred method.
2. **Add Cardamom:**
    - Stir the ground cardamom into the brewed coffee. Adjust the amount based on your taste preference.
3. **Sweeten (Optional):**
    - Add sugar if desired and stir until dissolved.
4. **Add Milk or Cream (Optional):**
    - Stir in milk or cream if you like your coffee creamy.
5. **Serve:**
    - Serve immediately.

Cardamom Coffee offers a unique and aromatic twist on traditional coffee, with a warm, spicy flavor from the cardamom.

Dalgona Coffee

Ingredients:

- 2 tbsp instant coffee
- 2 tbsp granulated sugar
- 2 tbsp hot water
- 1 cup milk (any type, hot or cold)

Instructions:

1. **Whip Coffee Mixture:**
    - In a mixing bowl, combine the instant coffee, sugar, and hot water.
    - Using a hand mixer or whisk, whip the mixture until it becomes light, fluffy, and forms stiff peaks (about 3-5 minutes).
2. **Prepare Milk:**
    - Heat the milk if you prefer a hot drink, or use it cold for an iced version.
3. **Assemble:**
    - Pour the milk into a glass.
4. **Top with Whipped Coffee:**
    - Spoon the whipped coffee mixture over the milk.
5. **Serve:**
    - Serve immediately. Stir before drinking to blend the coffee and milk.

Dalgona Coffee is a frothy, visually striking drink with a sweet, coffee flavor that's perfect for a cozy treat or a refreshing iced beverage.

Café Cubano

Ingredients:

- 2 shots of espresso (about 2 ounces)
- 2-3 tbsp sugar (adjust to taste)
- Optional: a small amount of hot water

Instructions:

1. **Prepare Espresso:**
    - Brew 2 shots of espresso using a fine coffee grind.
2. **Make the Sweetened Espresso:**
    - In a small cup or bowl, combine the sugar with a few drops of the freshly brewed espresso to create a paste.
    - Slowly add the remaining espresso to the paste while stirring vigorously. This creates a frothy, sweetened coffee.
3. **Serve:**
    - Pour the sweetened espresso into a small espresso cup.
4. **Optional:**
    - For a more traditional touch, you can dilute the coffee with a bit of hot water if desired.

Enjoy your Café Cubano, a strong, sweet Cuban coffee that's perfect for a quick, bold pick-me-up!

Turkish Coffee

Ingredients:

- 1 cup cold water
- 2 tbsp finely ground Turkish coffee (extra-fine grind)
- 1-2 tbsp sugar (optional, adjust to taste)
- Ground cardamom (optional, to taste)

Equipment:

- Turkish coffee pot (cezve or ibrik)
- Small cup (demitasse)

Instructions:

1. **Combine Ingredients:**
    - In a Turkish coffee pot, add the cold water.
    - Stir in the finely ground Turkish coffee and sugar (if using). Do not stir after this point.
2. **Heat the Coffee:**
    - Place the pot on low heat. Allow the coffee to heat slowly until it starts to froth. Do not stir during this process.
3. **Watch for Foam:**
    - As the coffee begins to froth and rise, remove the pot from the heat just before it boils over. Skim off some foam with a spoon and place it into your serving cup.
4. **Return and Finish:**
    - Return the pot to the heat and allow the coffee to froth again. Carefully pour the coffee into the cup, ensuring the foam rises to the top.
5. **Serve:**
    - Serve immediately. Turkish coffee is traditionally enjoyed without stirring. Let the grounds settle at the bottom of the cup before sipping.

Enjoy your Turkish Coffee, a rich, thick brew with a distinctive, strong flavor and a layer of frothy foam on top.

Vietnamese Iced Coffee

Ingredients:

- 2-3 tbsp coarsely ground Vietnamese coffee (or dark roast coffee)
- 2-3 tbsp sweetened condensed milk (adjust to taste)
- Ice cubes
- Hot water

Equipment:

- Vietnamese coffee filter (phin) or a drip coffee maker
- Glass

Instructions:

1. **Prepare Coffee Filter:**
   - Place 2-3 tablespoons of coarsely ground coffee into the Vietnamese coffee filter (phin).
2. **Brew Coffee:**
   - Pour a small amount of hot water over the grounds to bloom them.
   - Place the filter press on top of the grounds, then pour hot water (about 6 ounces) into the filter. Allow the coffee to drip through slowly. This takes about 4-5 minutes.
3. **Add Condensed Milk:**
   - While the coffee is still hot, stir in 2-3 tablespoons of sweetened condensed milk into a glass.
4. **Combine and Chill:**
   - Pour the brewed coffee over the condensed milk. Stir well to combine.
   - Add ice cubes to the glass and stir again.
5. **Serve:**
   - Serve immediately and enjoy the sweet, strong, and refreshing Vietnamese Iced Coffee!

This coffee combines the robust flavor of Vietnamese coffee with the sweetness of condensed milk, served over ice for a perfect pick-me-up.

Cold Brew Tonic

Ingredients:

- 1 cup cold brew coffee
- 1/2 cup tonic water
- Ice cubes
- Lemon or lime slice (for garnish)
- Optional: simple syrup or a splash of sweetener (adjust to taste)

Instructions:

1. **Prepare Cold Brew:**
    - Brew and chill cold brew coffee.
2. **Mix Ingredients:**
    - Fill a glass with ice cubes.
    - Pour the cold brew coffee over the ice.
3. **Add Tonic Water:**
    - Top with tonic water. Stir gently to combine.
4. **Optional Sweetener:**
    - If desired, add a splash of simple syrup or other sweetener to taste.
5. **Garnish:**
    - Garnish with a slice of lemon or lime.
6. **Serve:**
    - Serve immediately and enjoy your sparkling, refreshing Cold Brew Tonic!

This drink combines the smoothness of cold brew coffee with the effervescence of tonic water for a unique and invigorating beverage.

Coffee Lemonade

Ingredients:

- 1 cup brewed coffee (cooled)
- 1/2 cup freshly squeezed lemon juice
- 1/4 cup simple syrup (adjust to taste)
- 1 cup cold water
- Ice cubes
- Lemon slices (for garnish)

Instructions:

1. **Prepare Coffee:**
   - Brew and cool a cup of coffee.
2. **Mix Ingredients:**
   - In a pitcher, combine the cooled coffee, lemon juice, simple syrup, and cold water. Stir well.
3. **Serve:**
   - Fill glasses with ice cubes and pour the coffee lemonade over the ice.
4. **Garnish:**
   - Garnish with lemon slices.
5. **Enjoy:**
   - Serve immediately and enjoy the refreshing combination of coffee and lemonade!

This Coffee Lemonade blends the bold flavor of coffee with the tartness of lemonade for a unique and invigorating drink.

White Chocolate Mocha

Ingredients:

- 1 shot of espresso (about 1 ounce)
- 1 cup milk (any type)
- 2-3 tbsp white chocolate sauce or white chocolate chips
- Whipped cream (optional, for topping)
- White chocolate shavings (optional, for garnish)

Instructions:

1. **Prepare Espresso:**
    - Brew a shot of espresso and set it aside.
2. **Heat Milk and White Chocolate:**
    - In a small saucepan, heat the milk over medium heat until steaming but not boiling.
    - Stir in the white chocolate sauce or white chocolate chips until completely melted and the mixture is smooth.
3. **Combine Ingredients:**
    - Pour the hot milk and white chocolate mixture into a cup.
    - Add the brewed espresso and stir well.
4. **Optional Toppings:**
    - Top with whipped cream if desired.
    - Garnish with white chocolate shavings for an extra touch of indulgence.
5. **Serve:**
    - Serve immediately and enjoy the rich, sweet flavor of your White Chocolate Mocha!

This drink offers a creamy blend of espresso and white chocolate, topped with whipped cream for a decadent treat.

Spiced Coffee

Ingredients:

- 1 cup brewed coffee
- 1/4 tsp ground cinnamon
- 1/4 tsp ground nutmeg
- 1/4 tsp ground cloves (optional)
- 1-2 tbsp sugar or sweetener (adjust to taste)
- Milk or cream (optional, to taste)

Instructions:

1. **Brew Coffee:**
   - Brew a cup of coffee using your preferred method.
2. **Add Spices:**
   - Stir in the ground cinnamon, nutmeg, and cloves (if using). Mix well.
3. **Sweeten:**
   - Add sugar or your preferred sweetener to taste. Stir until dissolved.
4. **Add Milk or Cream (Optional):**
   - If desired, add milk or cream to taste for a creamier coffee.
5. **Serve:**
   - Serve immediately and enjoy the warm, spiced flavors.

This Spiced Coffee is perfect for adding a cozy touch to your coffee routine with aromatic spices and a touch of sweetness.

Coffee Egg Cream

Ingredients:

- 1/2 cup brewed coffee (cooled)
- 1/2 cup milk
- 1/4 cup seltzer water
- 2-3 tbsp chocolate syrup
- Ice (optional)

Instructions:

1. **Prepare Coffee:**
   - Brew and cool the coffee to room temperature.
2. **Combine Coffee and Milk:**
   - In a glass, mix the cooled coffee with the milk.
3. **Add Chocolate Syrup:**
   - Stir in the chocolate syrup until well blended.
4. **Add Seltzer Water:**
   - Slowly add the seltzer water to the mixture. Stir gently to combine.
5. **Serve:**
   - Add ice if desired and serve immediately.

Enjoy the unique, frothy blend of coffee and chocolate with a fizzy twist in this classic Coffee Egg Cream!

Coffee Smoothie

Ingredients:

- 1 cup brewed coffee (cooled)
- 1 banana
- 1/2 cup vanilla yogurt (or Greek yogurt)
- 1/2 cup milk (or a milk alternative)
- 1-2 tbsp honey or maple syrup (optional, to taste)
- Ice cubes

Instructions:

1. **Prepare Coffee:**
   - Brew and cool the coffee.
2. **Blend Ingredients:**
   - In a blender, combine the cooled coffee, banana, vanilla yogurt, milk, and honey or maple syrup if using.
   - Add a handful of ice cubes.
3. **Blend Until Smooth:**
   - Blend until the mixture is smooth and frothy.
4. **Serve:**
   - Pour into a glass and enjoy immediately.

This Coffee Smoothie is a deliciously creamy way to enjoy your coffee with a boost of banana and yogurt!

Pumpkin Spice Latte

Ingredients:

- 1 cup brewed espresso or strong coffee
- 1 cup milk (any type)
- 2 tbsp pumpkin puree
- 2 tbsp sugar or sweetener (adjust to taste)
- 1/2 tsp pumpkin pie spice (or a blend of cinnamon, nutmeg, and cloves)
- Whipped cream (optional, for topping)
- Extra pumpkin pie spice or cinnamon (optional, for garnish)

Instructions:

1. **Prepare Coffee:**
    - Brew a shot of espresso or a cup of strong coffee.
2. **Mix Pumpkin Spice Mixture:**
    - In a saucepan, combine the pumpkin puree, sugar, and pumpkin pie spice. Heat over medium heat, stirring constantly, until warmed and well mixed.
3. **Heat Milk:**
    - In a separate pan or using a steam wand, heat the milk until steaming. Froth if desired.
4. **Combine Ingredients:**
    - Stir the pumpkin spice mixture into the brewed espresso or coffee.
    - Pour the steamed milk over the coffee mixture and stir gently.
5. **Optional Toppings:**
    - Top with whipped cream and a sprinkle of extra pumpkin pie spice or cinnamon if desired.
6. **Serve:**
    - Serve immediately and enjoy your cozy Pumpkin Spice Latte!

This latte captures the warm, spicy flavors of fall with a creamy and comforting touch.

Peppermint Mocha

Ingredients:

- 1 shot of espresso (about 1 ounce) or 1/2 cup strong brewed coffee
- 1 cup milk (any type)
- 2 tbsp chocolate syrup or cocoa powder
- 1-2 tbsp peppermint syrup (adjust to taste) or 1/4 tsp peppermint extract
- Whipped cream (optional, for topping)
- Crushed peppermint candies (optional, for garnish)

Instructions:

1. **Prepare Coffee:**
   - Brew a shot of espresso or 1/2 cup of strong coffee.
2. **Heat Milk:**
   - In a saucepan or using a steam wand, heat the milk until steaming. Froth if desired.
3. **Mix Chocolate and Peppermint:**
   - In a separate cup, stir together the chocolate syrup or cocoa powder with the brewed coffee or espresso. Add the peppermint syrup or extract and mix well.
4. **Combine Ingredients:**
   - Pour the chocolate-peppermint coffee mixture into a cup.
   - Add the steamed milk and stir gently to combine.
5. **Optional Toppings:**
   - Top with whipped cream and sprinkle with crushed peppermint candies for a festive touch.
6. **Serve:**
   - Serve immediately and enjoy your holiday-themed Peppermint Mocha!

This drink blends the rich flavors of chocolate and peppermint with coffee, topped with whipped cream for a seasonal treat.

Hazelnut Cream Coffee

Ingredients:

- 1 cup brewed coffee
- 2 tbsp hazelnut syrup or hazelnut creamer
- 1/4 cup heavy cream (or milk for a lighter option)
- 1-2 tsp sugar (optional, adjust to taste)
- Whipped cream (optional, for topping)
- Chopped hazelnuts or cocoa powder (optional, for garnish)

Instructions:

1. **Prepare Coffee:**
   - Brew a cup of your favorite coffee.
2. **Flavor Coffee:**
   - Stir the hazelnut syrup or hazelnut creamer into the brewed coffee. Add sugar if desired and stir until dissolved.
3. **Prepare Cream:**
   - In a small bowl, whip the heavy cream until it forms soft peaks. If you prefer a lighter option, you can skip this step and use milk directly.
4. **Combine:**
   - Pour the flavored coffee into a cup.
5. **Top with Cream:**
   - Gently spoon or pipe the whipped cream on top of the coffee.
6. **Optional Garnish:**
   - Sprinkle with chopped hazelnuts or a dusting of cocoa powder for extra flavor and visual appeal.
7. **Serve:**
   - Serve immediately and enjoy the rich, nutty flavor of your Hazelnut Cream Coffee!

This coffee combines the nutty sweetness of hazelnut with a creamy topping for a luxurious coffee experience.

Cinnamon Roll Coffee

Ingredients:

- 1 cup brewed coffee
- 2 tbsp cinnamon syrup or 1/2 tsp ground cinnamon
- 1-2 tbsp vanilla syrup or extract
- 1/4 cup milk or cream
- Whipped cream (optional, for topping)
- Ground cinnamon or cinnamon sugar (optional, for garnish)

Instructions:

1. **Prepare Coffee:**
    - Brew a cup of your favorite coffee.
2. **Add Flavors:**
    - Stir in the cinnamon syrup or ground cinnamon and vanilla syrup or extract into the brewed coffee. Mix well.
3. **Heat and Froth Milk:**
    - Heat the milk or cream until steaming. Froth if desired.
4. **Combine:**
    - Pour the flavored coffee into a cup.
5. **Add Milk:**
    - Top with the steamed milk or cream.
6. **Optional Toppings:**
    - Add whipped cream on top if desired.
    - Garnish with a sprinkle of ground cinnamon or cinnamon sugar.
7. **Serve:**
    - Serve immediately and enjoy the warm, sweet flavor reminiscent of a cinnamon roll!

This coffee brings the delightful taste of cinnamon rolls to your cup with a creamy, spiced twist.

Maple Pecan Latte

Ingredients:

- 1 shot of espresso (about 1 ounce) or 1/2 cup strong brewed coffee
- 1 cup milk (any type)
- 2 tbsp maple syrup (adjust to taste)
- 1 tbsp pecan syrup or pecan extract (optional, for enhanced pecan flavor)
- Whipped cream (optional, for topping)
- Chopped pecans (optional, for garnish)

Instructions:

1. **Prepare Coffee:**
    - Brew a shot of espresso or 1/2 cup of strong coffee.
2. **Heat Milk:**
    - In a saucepan or using a steam wand, heat the milk until steaming. Froth if desired.
3. **Mix Flavors:**
    - In a cup, stir together the maple syrup and pecan syrup or extract if using.
4. **Combine Coffee and Flavors:**
    - Pour the brewed coffee or espresso into the cup with the maple and pecan mixture. Stir well to combine.
5. **Add Milk:**
    - Pour the steamed milk over the coffee mixture and stir gently.
6. **Optional Toppings:**
    - Top with whipped cream if desired.
    - Garnish with chopped pecans for added texture and flavor.
7. **Serve:**
    - Serve immediately and enjoy your Maple Pecan Latte!

This latte blends the rich flavors of maple and pecan for a sweet and nutty coffee treat.

Gingerbread Latte

Ingredients:

- 1 shot of espresso (about 1 ounce) or 1/2 cup strong brewed coffee
- 1 cup milk (any type)
- 2 tbsp gingerbread syrup or 1-2 tbsp gingerbread cookies crumbled
- 1/2 tsp ground ginger
- 1/4 tsp ground cinnamon
- Whipped cream (optional, for topping)
- Ground cinnamon or crushed gingerbread cookies (optional, for garnish)

Instructions:

1. **Prepare Coffee:**
   - Brew a shot of espresso or 1/2 cup of strong coffee.
2. **Heat Milk and Spice:**
   - In a saucepan, heat the milk until steaming.
   - Stir in the ground ginger and cinnamon. If using crumbled gingerbread cookies, add them to the milk as well, letting them steep and then strain if desired.
3. **Combine Flavors:**
   - Stir the gingerbread syrup into the brewed coffee or espresso.
4. **Add Milk:**
   - Pour the spiced milk over the coffee mixture. Stir gently to combine.
5. **Optional Toppings:**
   - Top with whipped cream if desired.
   - Garnish with a sprinkle of ground cinnamon or crushed gingerbread cookies.
6. **Serve:**
   - Serve immediately and enjoy the cozy, spiced flavor of your Gingerbread Latte!

This latte captures the warm, spicy notes of gingerbread in a creamy coffee drink perfect for the holiday season.

Mocha Nutella Coffee

Ingredients:

- 1 cup brewed coffee (hot)
- 2 tbsp Nutella (or another chocolate-hazelnut spread)
- 1-2 tbsp cocoa powder (optional, for extra chocolate richness)
- 1/4 cup milk (any type)
- Whipped cream (optional, for topping)
- Chopped hazelnuts or chocolate shavings (optional, for garnish)

Instructions:

1. **Prepare Coffee:**
   - Brew a cup of coffee.
2. **Mix Nutella:**
   - In a cup, stir the Nutella into the hot coffee until fully melted and well combined. If using cocoa powder for extra chocolate flavor, add it at this stage and mix until smooth.
3. **Heat and Froth Milk:**
   - In a small saucepan or using a steam wand, heat the milk until steaming. Froth if desired.
4. **Combine Ingredients:**
   - Pour the frothy milk into the coffee and Nutella mixture. Stir gently to combine.
5. **Optional Toppings:**
   - Top with whipped cream if desired.
   - Garnish with chopped hazelnuts or chocolate shavings for added texture and flavor.
6. **Serve:**
   - Serve immediately and enjoy the rich, nutty flavor of your Mocha Nutella Coffee!

This coffee combines the creamy, nutty taste of Nutella with the rich flavor of mocha, creating a decadent and indulgent drink.

Salted Caramel Latte

Ingredients:

- 1 shot of espresso (about 1 ounce) or 1/2 cup strong brewed coffee
- 1 cup milk (any type)
- 2-3 tbsp caramel sauce (plus extra for drizzling)
- A pinch of sea salt
- Whipped cream (optional, for topping)
- Extra sea salt or caramel drizzle (optional, for garnish)

Instructions:

1. **Prepare Coffee:**
   - Brew a shot of espresso or 1/2 cup of strong coffee.
2. **Heat Milk and Caramel:**
   - In a small saucepan, heat the milk until steaming.
   - Stir in 2-3 tablespoons of caramel sauce until fully blended and smooth.
3. **Combine Flavors:**
   - Pour the caramel-infused milk into the brewed coffee or espresso.
4. **Add Sea Salt:**
   - Stir in a pinch of sea salt. Taste and adjust if needed.
5. **Optional Toppings:**
   - Top with whipped cream if desired.
   - Drizzle additional caramel sauce over the whipped cream.
   - Sprinkle with a touch more sea salt for extra flavor.
6. **Serve:**
   - Serve immediately and enjoy the sweet, salty, and creamy flavors of your Salted Caramel Latte!

This latte combines the rich taste of caramel with a hint of sea salt for a deliciously balanced treat.

Espresso Lemonade

Ingredients:

- 1 shot of espresso (about 1 ounce)
- 1/2 cup freshly squeezed lemon juice
- 1/2 cup simple syrup (adjust to taste)
- 1 cup cold water
- Ice cubes
- Lemon slices (for garnish)

Instructions:

1. **Prepare Espresso:**
    - Brew a shot of espresso and let it cool.
2. **Mix Lemonade:**
    - In a pitcher, combine the lemon juice, simple syrup, and cold water. Stir well.
3. **Combine with Espresso:**
    - Add the cooled espresso to the lemonade mixture. Stir gently to combine.
4. **Serve:**
    - Fill glasses with ice cubes and pour the espresso lemonade over the ice.
5. **Garnish:**
    - Garnish with lemon slices.
6. **Enjoy:**
    - Serve immediately and enjoy the unique combination of coffee and citrus!

This drink offers a bold and refreshing twist on traditional lemonade with the added kick of espresso.

Café au Lait Affogato

Ingredients:

- 1 shot of espresso (about 1 ounce)
- 1/2 cup strong brewed coffee or café au lait
- 1-2 scoops vanilla ice cream
- Optional: chocolate shavings or caramel sauce for garnish

Instructions:

1. **Prepare Espresso and Coffee:**
    - Brew a shot of espresso and prepare 1/2 cup of strong brewed coffee or café au lait.
2. **Scoop Ice Cream:**
    - Place 1-2 scoops of vanilla ice cream into a serving glass or bowl.
3. **Combine Coffee:**
    - Pour the brewed coffee or café au lait over the ice cream.
4. **Add Espresso:**
    - Carefully pour the shot of espresso over the coffee and ice cream mixture.
5. **Optional Toppings:**
    - Garnish with chocolate shavings or a drizzle of caramel sauce if desired.
6. **Serve:**
    - Serve immediately and enjoy the indulgent blend of creamy ice cream and rich coffee!

This affogato combines the creamy sweetness of ice cream with the bold flavors of espresso and coffee, creating a delightful and decadent treat.

Coffee and Whiskey Cocktail

Ingredients:

- 1 oz brewed coffee (cooled)
- 1 1/2 oz whiskey (bourbon or your choice)
- 1/2 oz simple syrup (adjust to taste)
- 1/4 oz coffee liqueur (optional, for extra coffee flavor)
- Ice cubes
- Coffee beans or a lemon twist (optional, for garnish)

Instructions:

1. **Prepare Coffee:**
    - Brew coffee and let it cool to room temperature.
2. **Mix Cocktail:**
    - In a cocktail shaker, combine the cooled coffee, whiskey, simple syrup, and coffee liqueur if using.
3. **Shake:**
    - Add ice cubes to the shaker and shake well until chilled.
4. **Serve:**
    - Strain the mixture into a rocks glass filled with ice.
5. **Optional Garnish:**
    - Garnish with a few coffee beans or a lemon twist if desired.
6. **Enjoy:**
    - Serve immediately and savor the rich combination of coffee and whiskey.

This cocktail offers a robust mix of coffee and whiskey with a touch of sweetness, perfect for a sophisticated evening drink.

Maple Cinnamon Coffee

Ingredients:

- 1 cup brewed coffee
- 2 tbsp pure maple syrup (adjust to taste)
- 1/4 tsp ground cinnamon
- 1/4 cup milk or cream (optional)
- Whipped cream (optional, for topping)
- Extra ground cinnamon or cinnamon stick (optional, for garnish)

Instructions:

1. **Prepare Coffee:**
   - Brew a cup of your favorite coffee.
2. **Add Maple and Cinnamon:**
   - Stir in the maple syrup and ground cinnamon until well combined.
3. **Add Milk (Optional):**
   - If desired, heat and froth the milk or cream, then add it to the coffee mixture.
4. **Optional Toppings:**
   - Top with whipped cream if desired.
   - Garnish with a sprinkle of ground cinnamon or a cinnamon stick.
5. **Serve:**
   - Serve immediately and enjoy the sweet and spicy flavors of your Maple Cinnamon Coffee!

This coffee blends the warmth of cinnamon with the rich sweetness of maple for a comforting and flavorful drink.

Chocolate Coconut Coffee

Ingredients:

- 1 cup brewed coffee
- 2 tbsp chocolate syrup or cocoa powder
- 2 tbsp coconut milk or coconut cream
- 1-2 tbsp sweetened condensed milk or sugar (adjust to taste)
- Whipped cream (optional, for topping)
- Shredded coconut or chocolate shavings (optional, for garnish)

Instructions:

1. **Prepare Coffee:**
    - Brew a cup of your favorite coffee.
2. **Mix Chocolate and Sweetener:**
    - Stir in the chocolate syrup or cocoa powder until fully dissolved.
    - Add sweetened condensed milk or sugar, adjusting to taste.
3. **Add Coconut:**
    - Stir in the coconut milk or coconut cream. Mix well.
4. **Optional Toppings:**
    - Top with whipped cream if desired.
    - Garnish with shredded coconut or chocolate shavings for an extra touch.
5. **Serve:**
    - Serve immediately and enjoy the rich, tropical flavor of your Chocolate Coconut Coffee!

This coffee combines the indulgent flavors of chocolate and coconut for a deliciously creamy and tropical coffee experience.

Espresso Coconut Milk Latte

Ingredients:

- 1 shot of espresso (about 1 ounce) or 1/2 cup strong brewed coffee
- 1 cup coconut milk (canned or carton)
- 1-2 tbsp coconut syrup or sweetener (adjust to taste)
- 1/4 tsp vanilla extract (optional, for added flavor)
- Whipped cream (optional, for topping)
- Shredded coconut or toasted coconut flakes (optional, for garnish)

Instructions:

1. **Prepare Espresso:**
   - Brew a shot of espresso or 1/2 cup of strong coffee.
2. **Heat and Froth Coconut Milk:**
   - In a saucepan, heat the coconut milk until steaming but not boiling. If you have a steam wand, you can froth the coconut milk for a creamier texture.
3. **Add Sweetener:**
   - Stir in coconut syrup or sweetener to the hot coconut milk. Add vanilla extract if using.
4. **Combine Ingredients:**
   - Pour the brewed espresso into a cup.
   - Slowly add the steamed coconut milk over the espresso, holding back the foam with a spoon and then spooning it on top.
5. **Optional Toppings:**
   - Top with whipped cream if desired.
   - Garnish with shredded coconut or toasted coconut flakes.
6. **Serve:**
   - Serve immediately and enjoy your creamy Espresso Coconut Milk Latte!

This latte blends the rich flavor of espresso with the creamy, tropical taste of coconut milk, creating a delicious and dairy-free coffee drink.

www.ingramcontent.com/pod-product-compliance
Lightning Source LLC
LaVergne TN
LVHW061949070526
838199LV00060B/4046

9798330403516